Anna Magdalena's Notebook

Original manuscript in the Prussian State Library at Berlin

ANNA MAGDALENA'S NOTEBOOK

Johann Sebastian Bach married Anna Magdalena in 1721, while serving as Court Capellmeister at Anhalt-Cöthen. Bach's first wife had died in 1720, leaving 7 children. Anna Magdalena was a singer at the court, and for her beautiful soprano voice Bach wrote many of his most inspired arias. She enthusiastically participated in her husband's work; many of Johann Sebastian's compositions are preserved in her handwriting. Anna Magdalena fell heir to the job of raising Bach's children and bore him 13 more.

Anna Magdalena's Notebook was a gift from her husband, probably presented to her on her 24th birthday. Covered in green with a gold border, and complete with two locks and a red satin ribbon, it must have been a delight to the eye when it was new. The initials "A. M. B." and the date "1725" were stamped in the center of the cover in gold. Additional letters in ink were later added to the initials by Carl Philipp Emanuel Bach, to read "Anna Magdal Bach."

This notebook was to be filled with favorite selections of members of the Bach family circle, many in the handwriting of Anna Magdalena, some in the handwriting of J. S. Bach, and some in the script of younger members of the family. We are indebted to Anna Magdalena for collecting many of the simple and practical examples of light and elegant short selections in the "gallant style," which serve as an excellent introduction to music of the baroque period, particularly for young students. It is not known how many of these were compositions by J. S. Bach, but all of the pieces must have been enjoyed by the entire family.

A CD recording of the selections in *Anna Magdalena's Notebook*, performed by Valery Lloyd-Watts, is available separately (#16792).

Second Edition

Copyright © MCMXCII by Alfred Publishing Co., Inc.

Cover Painting by Toby Edward Rosenthal, 1870
Bach with His Family at Morning Devotion
Archiv für Kunst und Geschichte Berlin

ORNAMENTATION

Anna Magdalena's Notebook provides excellent opportunities for young students to learn the proper execution of baroque ornaments. It is unfortunate that so many editions of the Notebook contain incorrect ones. Those that are correct are often incorrectly realized; some editions show trills beginning on the principal note; some mention in the text the use of the inverted mordent, an ornament that did not exist in Bach's day.

This edition presents the original text, carefully prepared from the original autographs. The selections have been arranged in such an order as to introduce one ornament at a time. Suggestions for the correct realization of each ornament are provided by the editor, in light print.

In the discussion that follows, each of the ornaments found in the Notebook is taken up individually. This information is based on J. S. Bach's own table of ornaments in the CLAVIER-BÜCHLEIN VOR WILHELM FRIEDEMANN BACH and on information found in Carl Philipp Emanuel Bach's ESSAY ON THE TRUE ART OF PLAYING KEYBOARD INSTRUMENTS.

THE USE OF ORNAMENTS
IN ANNA MAGDALENA'S NOTEBOOK

1. THE TRILL

These symbols are used interchangeably to indicate a long or short trill.

All trills must begin on the upper note.

In C.P.E. Bach's ESSAY ON THE TRUE ART OF PLAYING KEYBOARD INSTRUMENTS, he states: "The trill begins on the tone above the principal note."

In the table of ornaments in the CLAVIER-BÜCHLEIN VOR WILHELM FRIEDEMANN BACH, Bach shows the following realization of a trill on a quarter note:

The number of repercussions in the trill is determined by the tempo of the selection as well as the time value of the note upon which it occurs.

The trill may come to rest on the principal note but at times may continue for the entire value of the note. The minimum number of notes in a trill is four.

Trills on longer notes may consume the entire time value of the note or may stop on the principal note on any beat or fraction of a beat.

2. THE TRILL WITH TERMINATION

The termination consists of two notes connected to the trill, at the same speed as the trill.

The trill requires a minimum of four notes and the termination consists of two notes:

The termination may be indicated by a sign added to the trill symbol ⚹ or ⚹ (these signs are not used in the selections we have chosen for this book) or it may be written out in notes following the trill, as it is in the Menuet on page 43, measure 21.

As the above example shows, the number of repercussions is optional and depends on the tempo of the selection as well as the skill and taste of the player. The values of the notes of the termination may be changed to agree with the notes of the trill.

According to the instructions of C.P.E. Bach, a termination may often be played, even when it is not indicated in the music. Most long trills are more effective with terminations. Short or long trills followed by the note one half-step or whole step above the principal note are usually effective with terminations.

In the Menuet on page 30, the trill in measure 4 is effective with a termination:

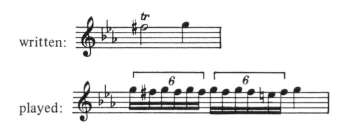

This trill may also be played with fewer or more repercussions.

3. THE MORDENT ⚹

The word "mordent" comes from the Latin verb "mordere" (to bite). This describes the incisive quality of the mordent, which is played very quickly. It contributes brilliance to the music.

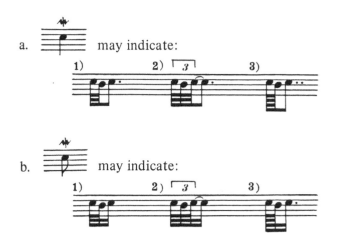

Regardless of the time-values shown in the realizations, it is usually best to play mordents as quickly as possible. In extremely rapid passages, the mordent is sometimes played by striking both notes simultaneously, then immediately releasing the lower note (C.P.E. Bach, *ESSAY*).

4. THE APPOGGIATURA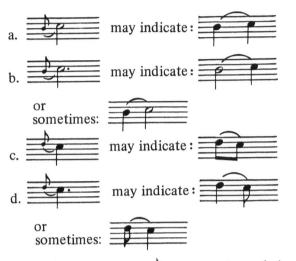

These small notes are always played ON THE BEAT. The appoggiatura takes half the time value of the following note, except when the following note is dotted. It then usually takes two-thirds of the value of the note.

a. may indicate:

b. may indicate:

or sometimes:

c. may indicate:

d. may indicate:

or sometimes:

The modern grace note ♪ was not used in the baroque period.

When an appoggiatura occurs before a trill and the small note is the same as the upper note of the trill, the ornament is called a PREPARED TRILL. In this case the appoggiatura is treated as a prolongation of the starting note of the trill.

An example appears in the March on page 18, measure 7:

written: played:

5. THE SCHLEIFER ~

This ornament is called the "slide." This type of schleifer adds the two lower neighboring tones before the principal note, which follows the sign. The ornament is played ON THE BEAT, and the value of the added notes are subtracted from the principal note. It is always played rapidly.

There is one example of the schleifer in Anna Magdalena's Notebook. It occurs in the Menuet on page 26, measure 6.

written:

played:

THE SIMPLIFICATION
OR OMISSION OF ORNAMENTS

Some teachers may prefer to have the student learn these selections without the ornaments so the pieces fall more easily into the student's grade level. There is no objection to this, and if the ornaments can be added later, this practice may result in a more thorough understanding of the functions of baroque ornamentation, which was not only to embellish but to add interesting dissonances and harmonic interest.

It is, of course, equally acceptable to retain the simpler ornaments and omit the more difficult ones. In the CLAVIER-BÜCHLEIN VOR WILHELM FRIEDEMANN BACH there is evidence that J. S. Bach himself allowed his young son to omit some ornaments in the left hand part which he undoubtedly would have played himself, but being aware of his son's limitations at the time, he preferred to have the pieces played in a simplified form rather than to eliminate them entirely. He even provided Wilhelm Friedemann with greatly simplified versions of several preludes from the WELL-TEMPERED CLAVIER.

One word of caution is in order, concerning the simplification of ornaments. The short trill should NEVER be replaced by a so-called "upper mordent." In substituting the "inverted" or "upper" mordent for a trill, one loses almost completely the dissonant function of the baroque trill, which was similar to that of the appoggiatura. In Carl Philipp Emanuel Bach's ESSAY ON THE TRUE ART OF PLAYING KEYBOARD INSTRUMENTS he makes the following recommendation: "In very rapid tempos the effect of a trill can be achieved through the use of an appoggiatura." To illustrate this, he gives the following example:

written:

simplification:

The student should be reminded that the three symbols ~, ~~, and *tr* were used synonymously by Bach.

THE ADDITION OF ORNAMENTS

In the baroque period, any musician who did not add a few of his own ornaments to the selections he played was considered very dull and unimaginative. This practice has been frowned on in recent years, but there are no grounds for this attitude, particularly in playing the music from the Anna Magdalena Notebook. Some ornaments are omitted because their use was rather obvious.

An example appears on page 16. Since an appoggiatura is used in measure 4, an appoggiatura may be added when similar passages occur in measures 13 and 25. Examples of added trills are found in the footnotes on pages 26 and 27, and the student should be encouraged to discover similar cadences in other pieces in this book to which trills may be added.

DOTTED RHYTHMS IN BAROQUE MUSIC

In the baroque period, the value of a dot after a note was not always strictly observed. The dot was often lengthened and the note used in combination with it was shortened.

This interpretation often adds the brilliance and vigor that are characteristic of much of the music of the period.

There are a number of passages in Anna Magdalena's

Notebook that gain added charm when the dot is exaggerated. One example is the first measure of the Polonaise on page 7.

DYNAMICS, TEMPOS AND PHRASING

There are no indications of dynamics and tempos in any of the music in Anna Magdalena's Notebook. A few slurs occur, many of which are in the songs and serve the purpose of indicating two or more notes to be sung on one syllable of the text.

The dynamics, tempo indications and slurs in light print have been added by the editor and may be observed according to the discretion of the teacher or student.

ACKNOWLEDGMENT

I would like to express my thanks to Judith Simon Linder for her valuable assistance in the research necessary for the realization of this edition, and for her help in preparing the manuscript.

ARIA
ENLIGHTENING THOUGHTS OF A TOBACCO SMOKER
(ERBAULICHE GEDANKEN EINES TABAKRAUCHERS)

Moderato M. M. ♩ = 72 - 76

BWV 515

This aria was probably a popular song of its day. The text appears on page 46.

POLONAISE

BWV Anhang 119

Allegro moderato M.M. ♩ = 92 - 100

ⓐ The dotted rhythm may be exaggerated in this and the 5th measure. The first measure would be played:

See the discussion of **DOTTED RHYTHMS IN BAROQUE MUSIC** on page 5.

MENUET

Un poco animato M. M. ♩ = 112 - 126

BWV Anhang 116

Although the menuet was sometimes a rather slow and stately dance, this was not always so. Some 18th century musicians describe it as "gay and very quick" (Jean Jacques Rousseau), "very lively" (Brossard). Quantz gives a tempo of two quarter notes for each beat of the human pulse, or something at least as fast as M. M. ♩ = 120.

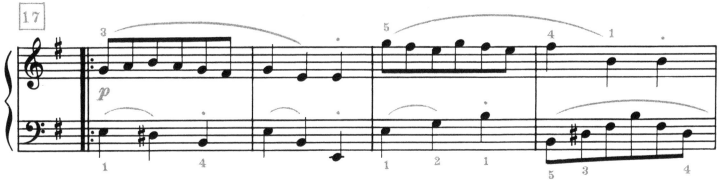

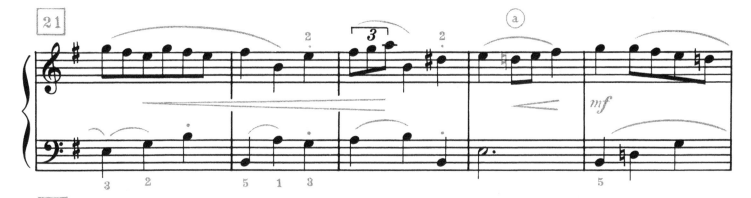

ⓐ Most modern editions have D♯ here. The sharp does not appear in the original manuscript.

MUSETTE

Moderato M.M. ♩ = 60 - 69

BWV Anhang 126

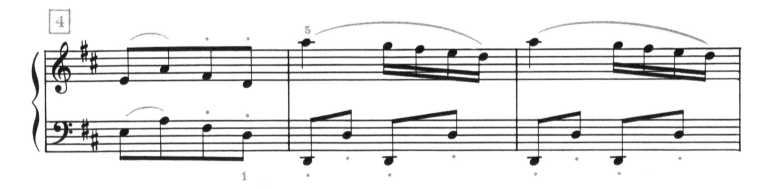

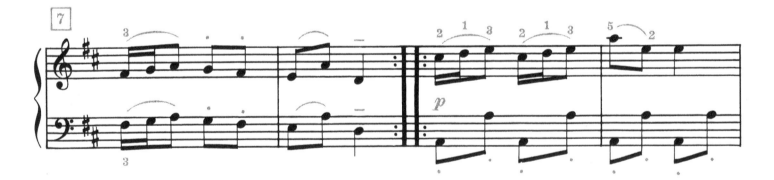

A musette is an instrument of the bagpipe family. Selections titled "Musette" were originally imitations of that instrument. The melody of this selection resembles those played by the bagpipe and the basses almost have a droning effect. This style of bass writing, with repeated octaves, was called "MURKY BASS."

Quantz suggested a "caressing expression" for the musette and warned against playing too fast.

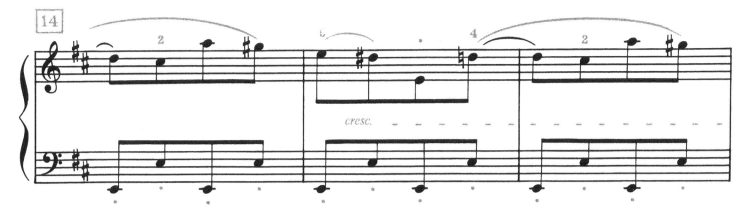

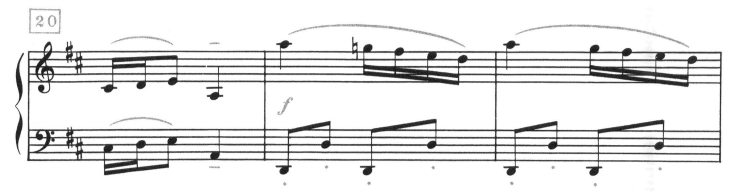

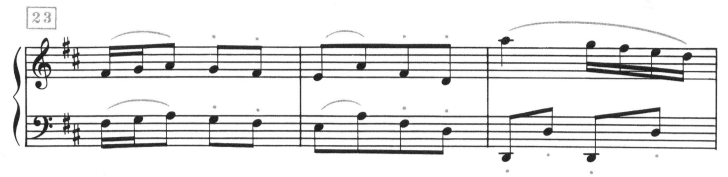

CHORALE
BE CONTENT
(GIB DICH ZUFRIEDEN)

BWV 512

The text of this chorale appears on page 47.

(a) The small slurs in dark print appear in the original manuscript to indicate notes that were sung on one syllable of a word in the text.

(b) The fermata ⌢ was often used in choral pieces to indicate the end of a line of the text, rather than a pause or prolongation of the note.

(c) See pages 2 & 3 for a discussion of the TRILL. This trill may have more repercussions, if desired.

CHORALE
DO WITH ME AS THOU WILT
(SCHAFF'S MIT MIR)

BWV 514

The text of this chorale appears on page 47.

This selection must have been used by Anna Magdalena to teach someone who could not read music well. In the original manuscript in Anna Magdalena's handwriting, the letter-names are written above or below each note, up to the first double bar.

Only the upper and lower voices appear in the manuscript, but figures appear above the bass notes, indicating that additional harmonies at certain intervals above the basses are to be added. This type of indication was called "figured bass."

MENUET

Moderato M.M. ♩ = 66 - 72

BWV Anhang 118

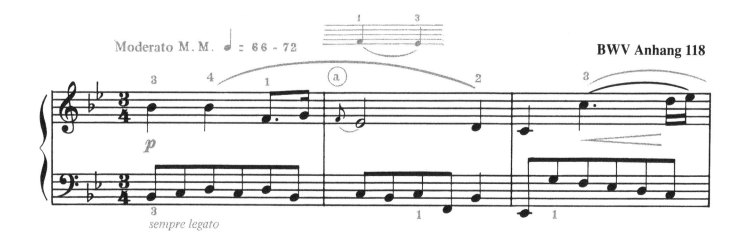

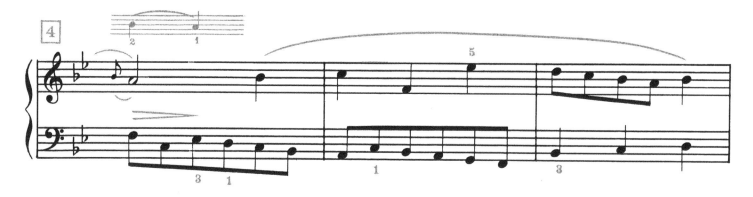

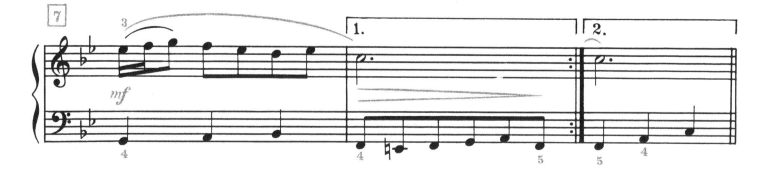

ⓐ This ornament is called an **APPOGGIATURA**. See page 4.
ⓑ This is an example of a trill with a written termination. See page 3.

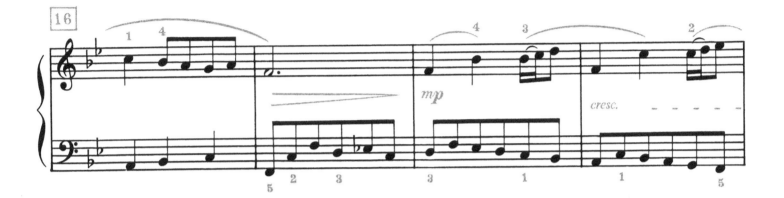

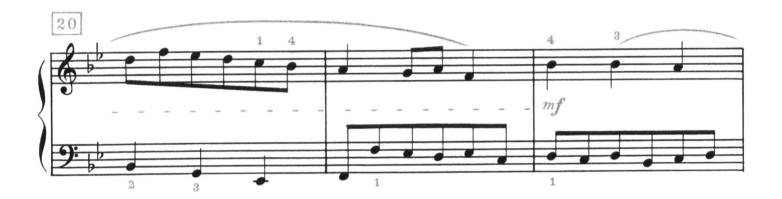

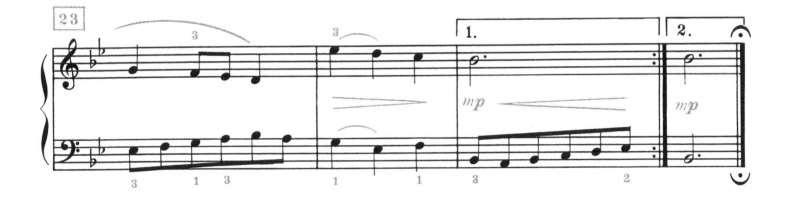

16

MENUET
(FAIT PAR MONS. BÖHM)

No BWV number

ⓐ The French words "Fait par Mons. Böhm" mean "Composed by Mr. Böhm." Georg Böhm (1661 - 1733) was a noted organist at Luneburg, Germany. In his youth, J. S. Bach may have studied with him. Some of Bach's early compositions show the influence of Böhm's style.

ⓑ The appoggiatura before a dotted note usually receives two-thirds of the value of the note, but in some cases it may receive only one-third of its value. It is usually wise to play it both ways and select the one that sounds best.

ⓒ An appoggiatura may be added here. See THE ADDITION OF ORNAMENTS on page 5.

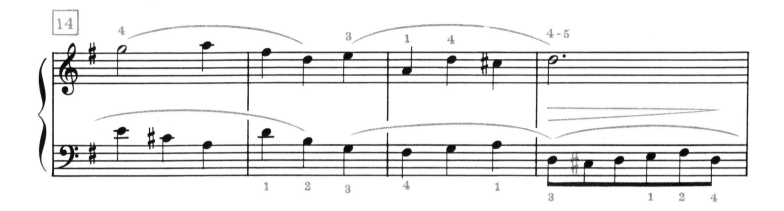

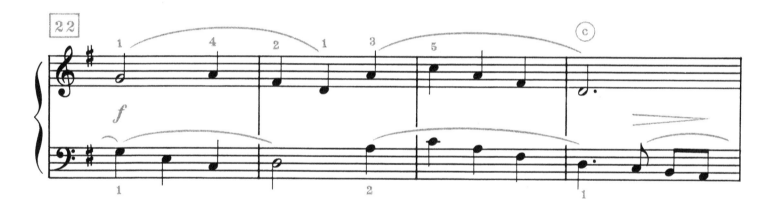

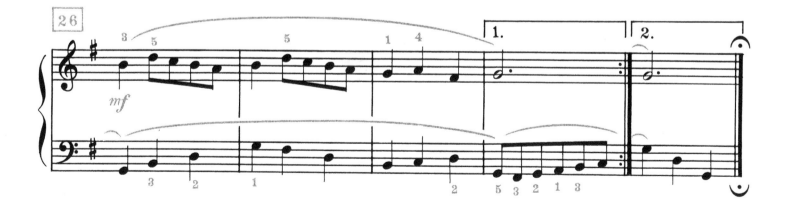

ⓒ See ⓒ on the previous page.

MARCH

Carl Philipp Emanuel Bach
(1714–1788)
BWV Anhang 122

Moderate march tempo M. M. ♩ = 120-126

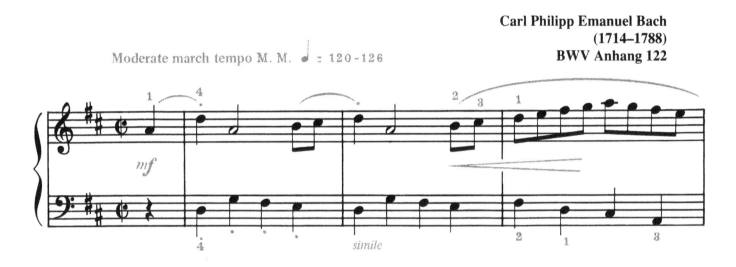

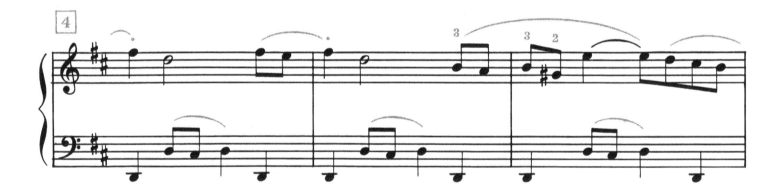

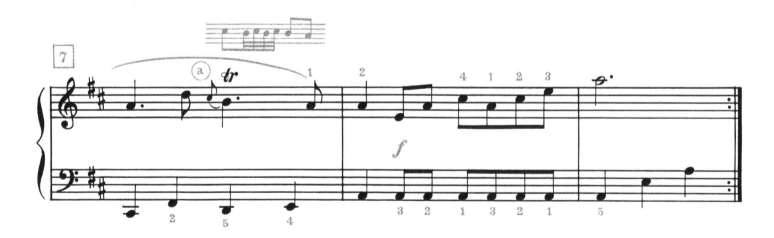

ⓐ Here two ornaments are combined: the APPOGGIATURA and TRILL. See page 4.

The dotted note may be prolonged:

See page 5 for a discussion of DOTTED RHYTHMS IN BAROQUE MUSIC.

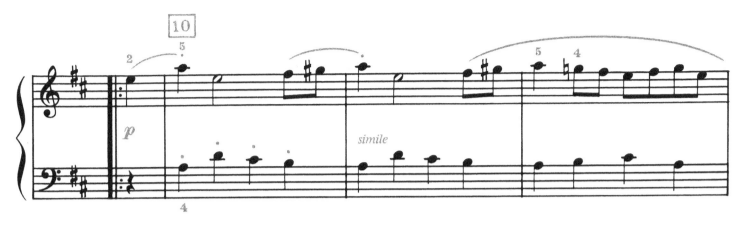

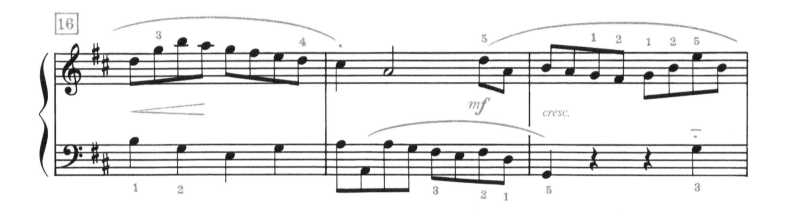

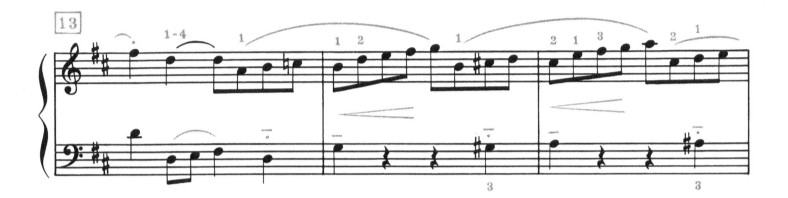

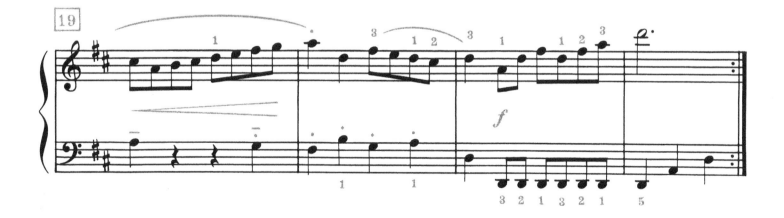

MENUET

Attr. to Christian Pezold (Petzold)
(1677–1733)
BWV Anhang 114

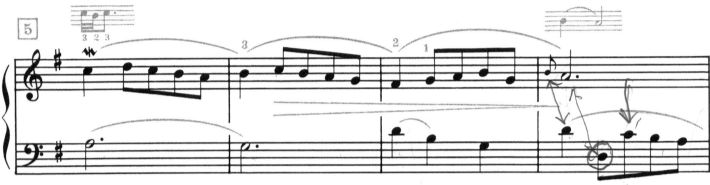

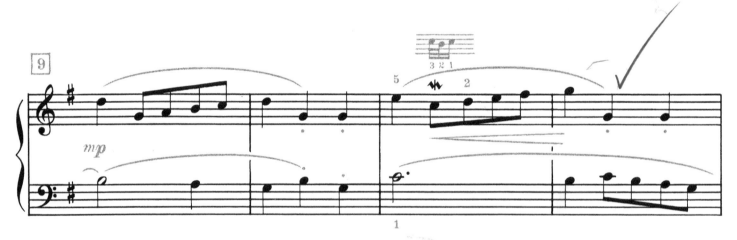

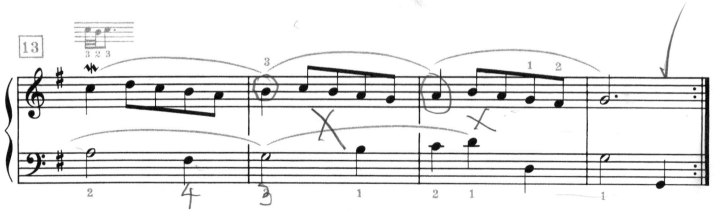

In the baroque period, menuets were often played in pairs. This menuet may be followed immediately by the menuet on page 22. after which it may be played again without repeats, according to the custom of the period.
ⓐ This ornament is called a MORDENT. See the discussion on page 3.

COUNT

COUNT

21

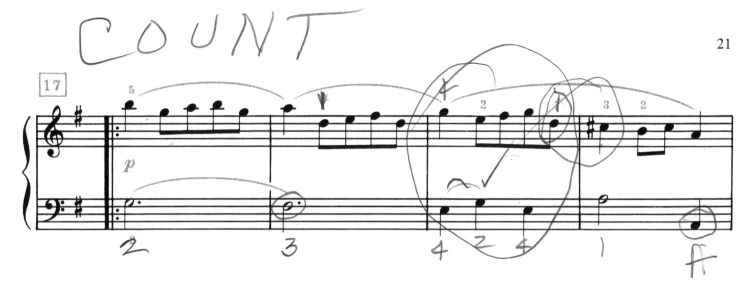

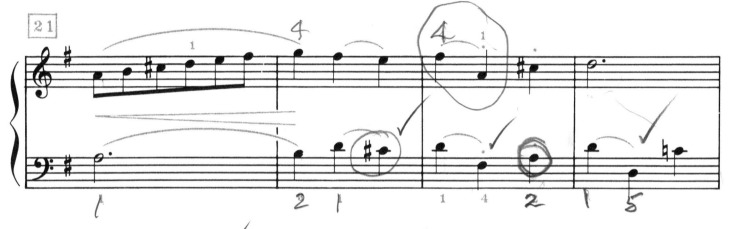

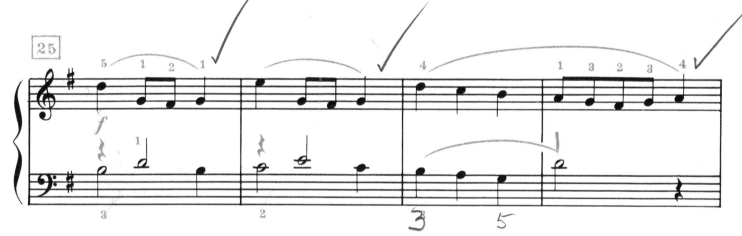

MENUET

Attr. to Christian Pezold
BWV Anhang 115

This menuet may be used to follow the menuet on page 20. See the footnote on that page.

23

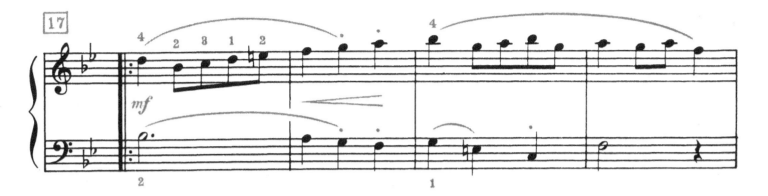

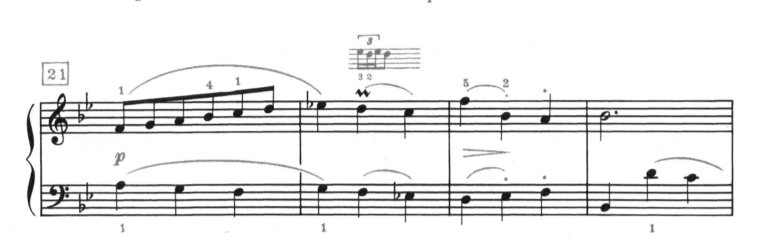

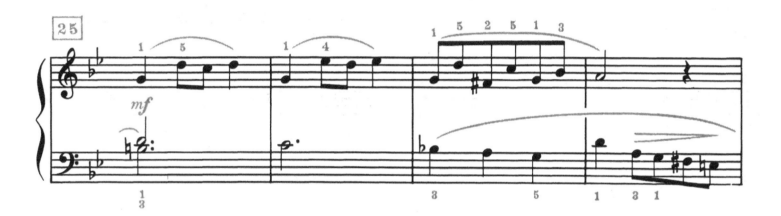

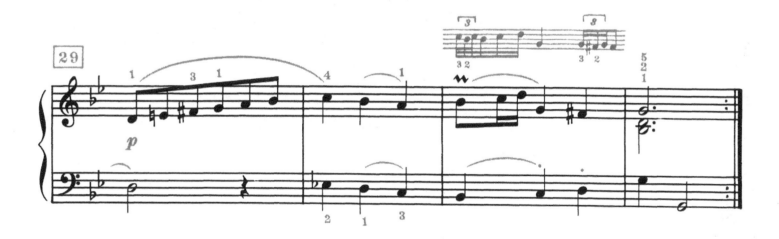

MARCH

Attr. to **Carl Philipp Emanuel Bach**
BWV Anhang 124

ⓐ The value of the dot may be exaggerated and the ornament played as follows:

See the explanation of **DOTTED RHYTHMS IN THE BAROQUE PERIOD**, page 5.

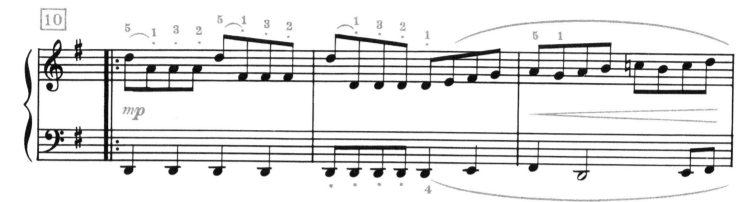

(b) May be played:

See footnote (a) on the previous page.

MENUET

Allegro moderato M.M. ♩ = 108-120

BWV Anhang 132

(a) This ornament is called a SCHLEIFER. See page 4.
(b) Baroque musicians often added trills at the cadences (closing notes of a composition or section of a composition). A trill with termination is effective here and may be played thus:

See THE ADDITION OF ORNAMENTS, page 5.

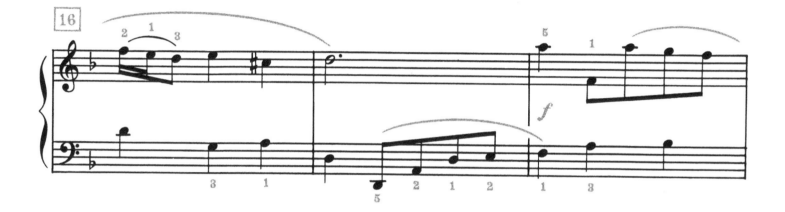

ⓒ A trill with termination may be added at the cadence:
See footnote ⓑ on the previous page.

MARCH

BWV Anhang 127

Allegro giocoso M. M. ♩ = 116-126

ⓐ The trill may have more repercussions; for example:

A termination may also be used:

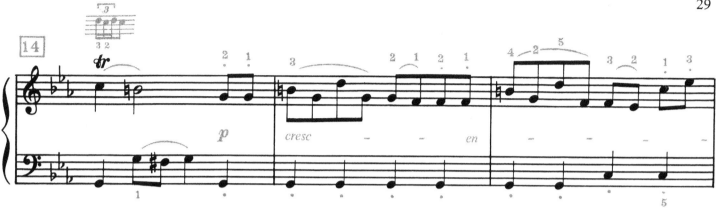

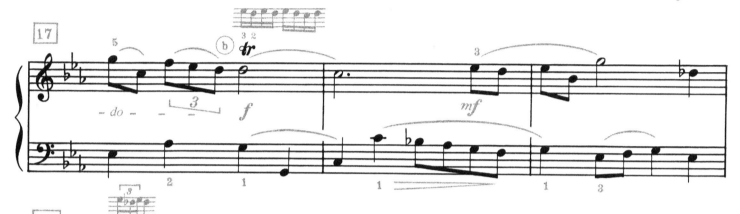

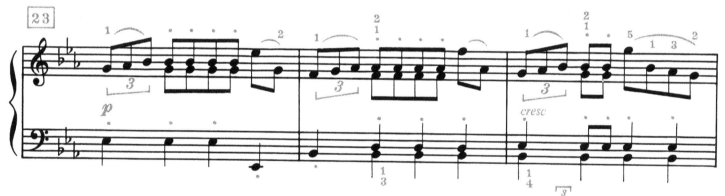

ⓑ The trill may be played with more repercussions.

ⓒ The trill may have more repercussions. It may also have a termination. See footnote ⓐ on the previous page.

MENUET

Allegro moderato M. M. ♩ = 108 - 120

BWV Anhang 121

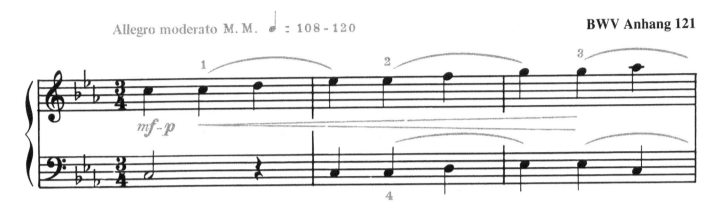

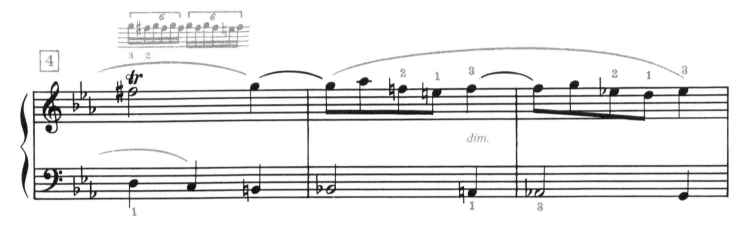

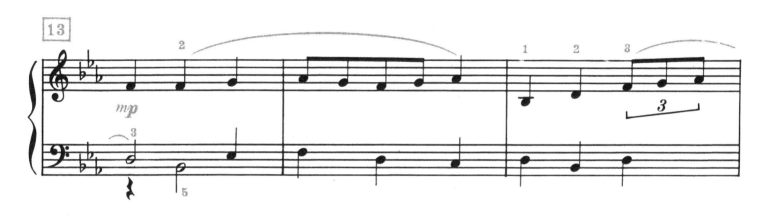

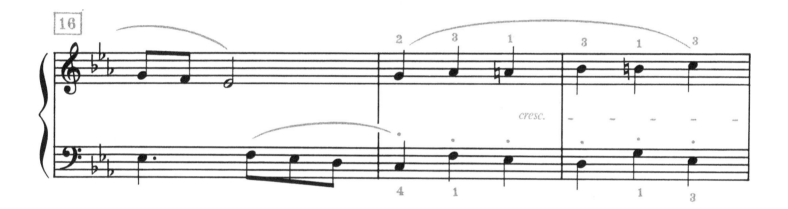

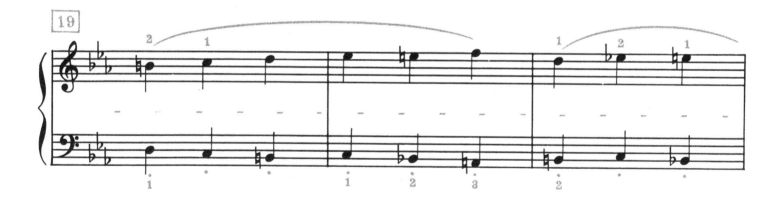

PRELUDE

BWV 846

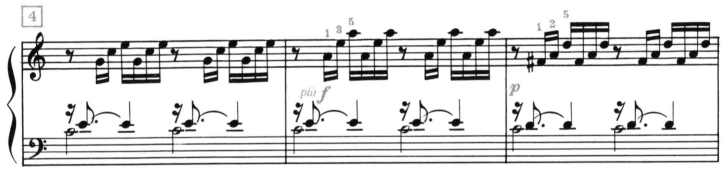

This is one of J. S. Bach's most famous compositions. It is the first prelude in his WELL-TEMPERED CLAVIER, Volume I. This book contains 24 preludes and fugues, one in each major and minor key, and helped to firmly establish the modern system of tempered tuning of keyboard instruments.

ⓐ Measures 16 through 20 (inclusive) are omitted from the original manuscript but appear in the Well-Tempered Clavier.

ⓑ Many editions add an extra measure between measures 22 and 23, which is not to be found in any of Bach's autographs.

ARIA
WHEN THOU ART NEAR
(BIST DU BEI MIR)

Attr. to Gottfried Heinrich Stölzel
(1690–1749)
BWV 508

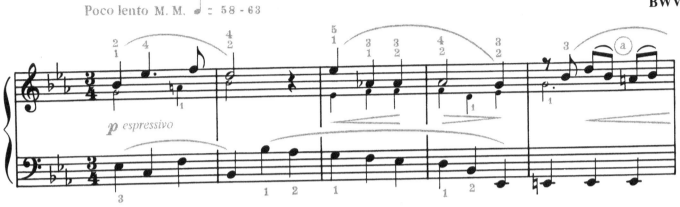

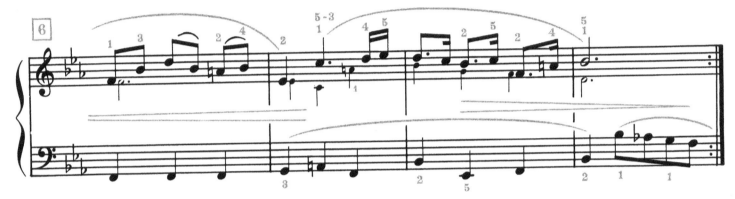

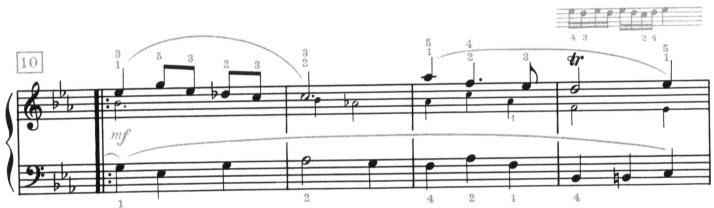

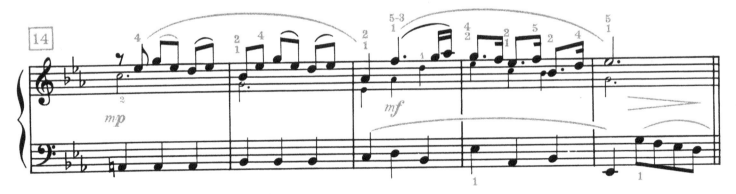

The words to this famous song appear on page 47.

The small notes represent a simple harmonization by the editor. The original manuscript contains only the soprano and bass voices.

ⓐ Natural signs are missing from the A's in measures 5, 6, 8, 22, 32, 33, 34 and 35 of the original manuscript.

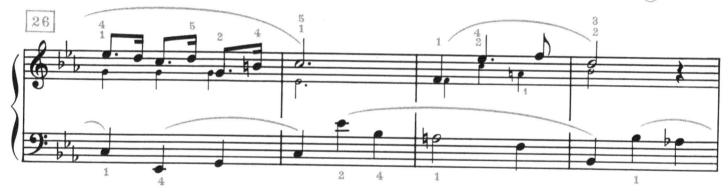

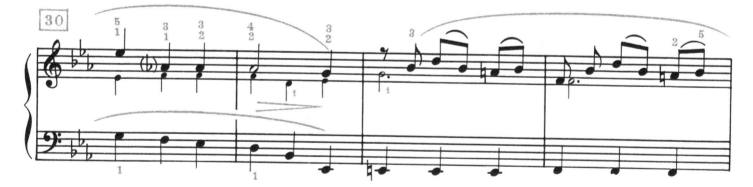

ⓑ The original manuscript has A♭ in the first space. B♮ appears in most modern editions.

MENUET

BWV Anhang 113

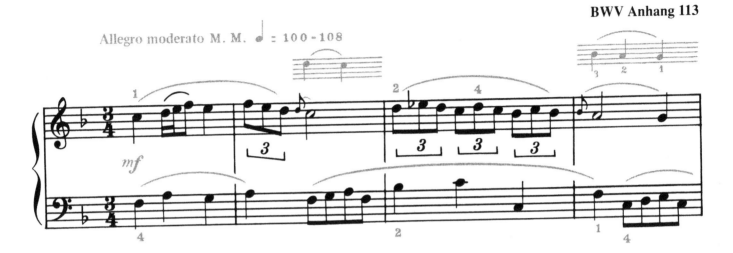

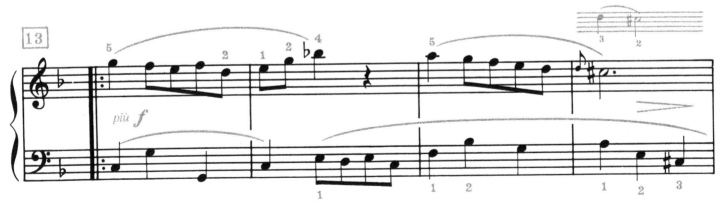

ⓐ The trill may be simplified by substituting an appoggiatura. See page 4.

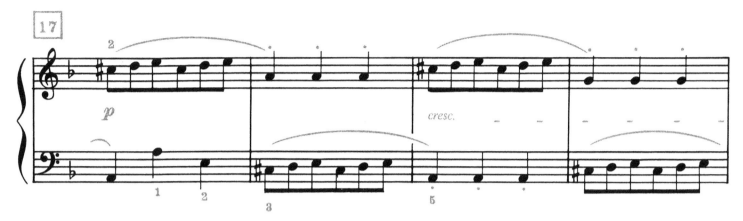

POLONAISE

Carl Philipp Emanuel Bach
BWV Anhang 125

Allegro moderato M.M. ♩ = 88-96

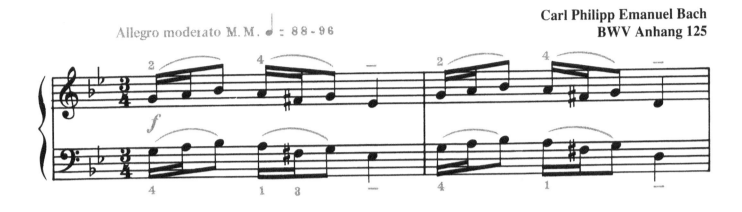

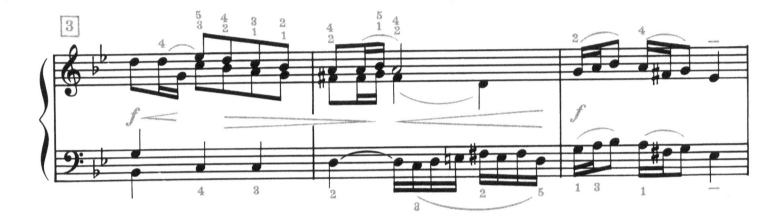

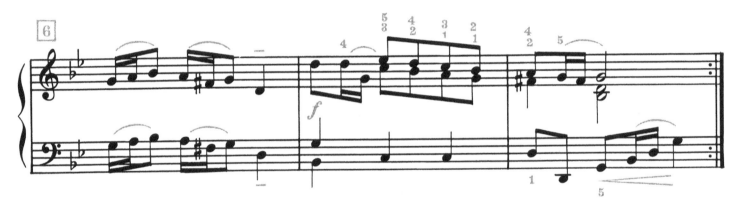

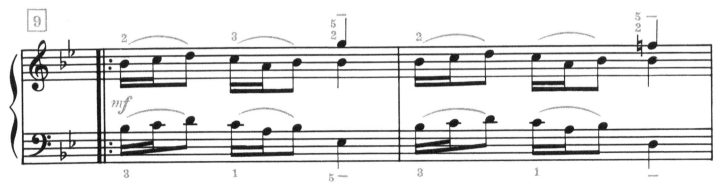

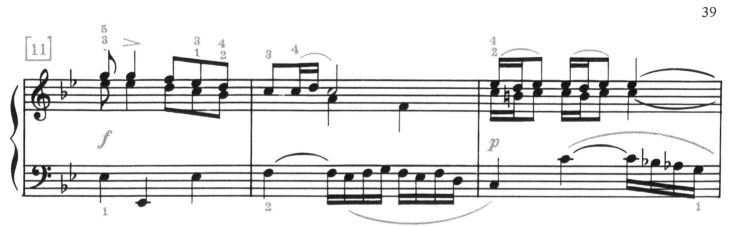

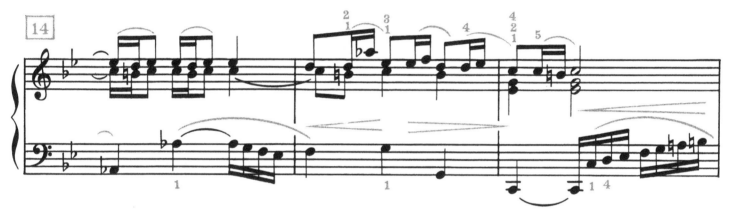

POLONAISE

Attr. to Carl Philipp Emanuel Bach
BWV Anhang 123

Allegro moderato e maestoso M.M. ♩ = 80 - 86

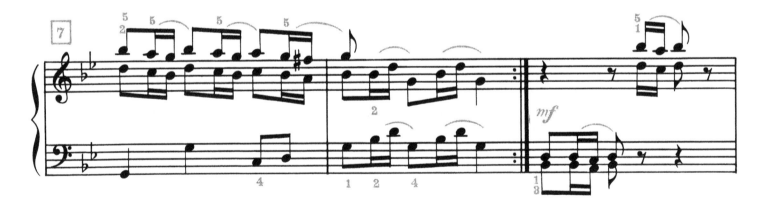

41

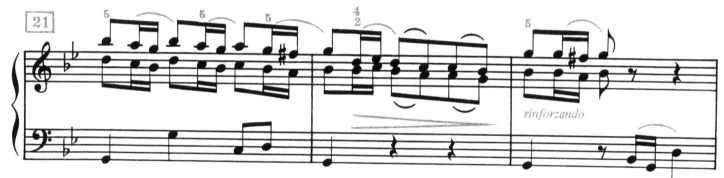

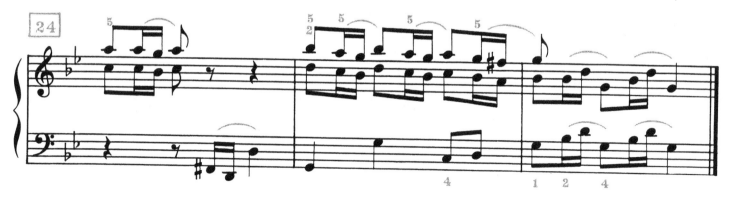

MENUET

BWV Anhang 120

Allegretto M. M. ♩ = 108 - 120

ⓐ

5

9

13

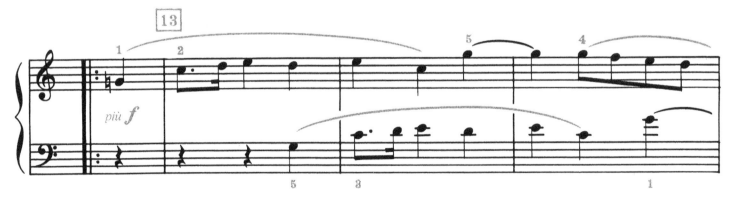

ⓐ The dotted notes in this and similar measures may be exaggerated. See the discussion of DOTTED RHYTHMS IN BAROQUE MUSIC, page 5.

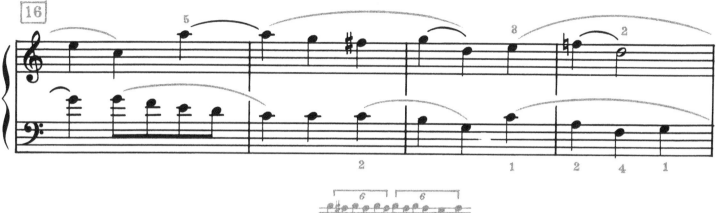

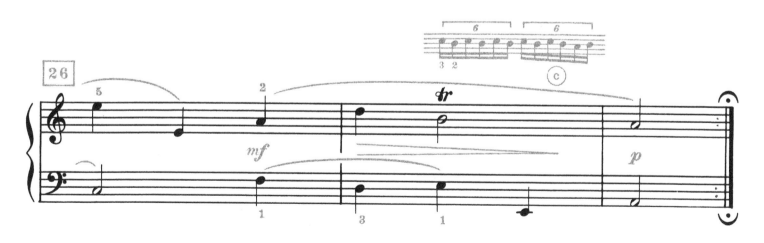

ⓑ In playing these trills, the terminations are played at the same speed as the notes of the trill, regardless of their written values.

ⓒ This is an example of an added termination, not indicated in the music. See the discussion of the TRILL WITH TERMINATION, page 3.

POLONAISE

Attr. to Johann Adolf Hasse
(1699–1783)
BWV Anhang 130

ⓐ Here the ornamentation combines an appoggiatura with a mordent. The appoggiatura gets half the value of the note, delaying the mordent until the third beat of the measure.

ⓑ The appoggiatura was often written as a small quarter note. In this case, the meaning is the same as if it were written as a small eighth note. The appoggiatura delays the trill until the third beat.

SONG TEXTS

Enlightening Thoughts of a Tobacco Smoker/pg.6
ERBAULICHE GEDANKEN EINES TABAKRAUCHERS

Whenever I pick up my tobacco-pipe,
Stuffed with good tobacco
For pleasure and pastime,
It gives me a sad impression —
And leads to the conclusion
That I resemble it in many ways.

The pipe was made from clay and earth
And so was I.
One day I will be earth again —
It often falls from the hand
And breaks before you know,
My destiny is the same.

The pipe is usually not colored;
It remains white. So therefore,
One day when I am dying
My body will turn pale.
Once buried it becomes black, just like
A pipe that has been used for a long time.

When the pipe is lit,
One sees the smoke disappear instantly
In the free air,
Leaving nothing but ashes behind.
The glory of all mankind is consumed
And the body turns to dust.

So often it happens while smoking,
That the stuffer is not handy,
And instead the finger is used.
Then I wonder when I burn myself,
If the ashes make such pain
How hot will it be in Hades?

Since such is the case,
From my tobacco I can always
Erect enlightening thoughts.
Therefore, in comfort I smoke
On land, at sea and at home
My little pipe, with devotion.

So oft ich meine Tobacks-Pfeife,
Mit gutem Knaster angefüllt,
Zur Lust und Zeitvertreib ergreife,
So gibt sie mir ein Trauerbild —
Und füget diese Lehre bei,
Dass ich derselben ähnlich sei.

Die Pfeife stammt von Thon und Erde,
Auch ich bin gleichfalls draus gemacht.
Auch ich muss einst zur Erde werden —
Sie fällt und bricht, eh ihr's gedacht,
Mir oftmals in der Hand entzwei,
Mein Schicksal ist auch einerlei.

Die Pfeife pflegt man nicht zu färben,
Sie bleibet weiss. Also der Schluss,
Dass ich auch dermaleins im Sterben
Dem Leibe nach erblassen muss.
Im Grabe wird der Körper auch —
So schwarz, wie sie nach langem Brauch.

Wenn man die Pfeife angezündet,
So sieht man, wie im Augenblick
Der Rauch in freier Luft verschwindet,
Nichts als die Asche bleibt zurück.
So wird des Menschen Ruhm verzehrt
Und dessen Leib in Staub verkehrt.

Wie oft geschieht's nicht bei dem Rauchen,
Dass, wenn der Stopfer nicht zur Hand,
Man pflegt den Finger zu gebrauchen.
Dann denk ich, wenn ich mich verbrannt:
O, macht die Kohle solche Pein,
Wie heiss mag erst die Hölle sein?

Ich kann bei so gestalten Sachen
Mir bei dem Toback jederzeit
Erbauliche Gedanken machen.
Drum schmauch ich voll Zufriedenheit
Zu Land, zu Wasser und zu Haus
Mein Pfeifchen stets in Andacht aus.

Be Content/pg.12
GIB DICH ZUFRIEDEN

Be content and silent
In the God of your life.

In Him rests the fullness of joy,
Without Him your works are in vain.

He is thy fountain and thy sun,
Shining brightly each day for your delight.
Be content, be content.

Gib dich zufrieden, und sei stille
In dem Gotte deines Lebens.

In Ihm ruht aller Freuden Fülle,
Ohn' Ihn mühst du dich vergebens.

Er ist dein Quell und deine Sonne,
Scheint täglich hell zu deiner Wonne.
Gib dich zufrieden, zufrieden.

Do With Me As Thou Wilt/pg.13
SCHAFF'S MIT MIR

Do with me, God, as Thou wilt,
So be it.

Thou wilt fulfill my wishes
According to Thy wisdom.

Thou art my Father, Thou wilt care for me,
My faith is in Thee.

Schaff's mit mir, Gott, nach deinem Willen,
Dir sei es alles heimgestellt.

Du wirst mein Wünschen so erfüllen,
Wie's deiner Weisheit wohlgefällt.

Du bist mein Vater, du wirst mich versorgen,
Darauf hoffe ich.

When Thou Art Near/pg.34
BIST DU BEI MIR

Measures 1 — 9 and
Measures 10 — 18:

> When thou are near
> I go with joy
> To death and to my rest,
> To death and to my rest.

Measures 19 — 36:

> Oh how joyous
> Would my end be,
> If your fair hands
> Would close my faithful eyes.

Measures 1 — 9 and
Measures 10 — 18:

> Bist du bei mir
> Geh ich mit Freuden
> Zum Sterben und zu meiner Ruh,
> Zum Sterben und zu meiner Ruh.

Measures 19 — 36:

> Ach, wie vergnügt
> Wär so mein Ende,
> Es drückten deine schönen Hände
> Mir die getreuen Augen zu.

THEMATIC INDEX